This Book Belongs to;
ISBN: 9798732563184

It is a bright Saturday and today is going to take a
different turn for mysterious Muri

The midday sun has just risen in the sky and Ben has decided
to do some work in his little garden.

Muri is in the living room relaxing.
He is watching cartoons on the TV.

Ben comes out from his room to meet him.

"Muri, will you come to the garden with me?" Ben asks, "I am sure you will like it," he adds, trying to convince Muri.

"Yes!" exclaims Muri in excitement. He wastes no time turning off the TV set.

Muri is excited. He wants to have his first gardening experience.

They walk to the store close to the back door and get the basic gardening tools that they need for the work.

Ben is not doing any planting today. He only wants to water the plants and prune the beautiful flowers.

So they only get the weeder, watering can, pruning shears, rake, and wheelbarrow.

Ben takes a gardening hat for himself and hands one to Muri.

He puts on his hat and watches Muri do the same. He cannot help but laugh as the hat covers Muri's entire head.

Then Ben takes a pair of gardening gloves and puts
them on as they head towards the garden.

Muri wishes he has the fingers to use gloves. He smiles to
himself as they head toward the garden.

Soon, they get to the garden and are getting set for work when Muri sees a scarecrow at the edge of the garden.

He is scared and shivering, so he moves close to Ben and points to the scarecrow. Ben sees what Muri is afraid of and begins to laugh.

"Oh, that?" begins Ben, "It's a scarecrow; I made it to scare the birds away from my little garden," he concludes, smiling at Muri.

Muri becomes settled and they set to work.

First, they look around the plants and flowers to check for weeds. "Let's get rid of the weeds, Muri," Ben says, showing him the weeds, "But we must be careful not to harm the plants," he adds.

Some weeds are so close to the plants and flowers that the weeder
might harm the plants. So we have to hand-pick these weeds safely.

The moment they are done weeding the garden, Ben takes the pruning shears and prunes the flowers. Then they rake the dirt and pack everything into the wheelbarrow in front of the garden. Ben pushes the wheelbarrow to dispose of the weeds.

They are done keeping the
garden clean and healthy for
the plants and flowers. It is
time to give the plants life.
Water is life for them.

Ben shows Muri how to water the plants and flowers without applying too much water to them. He waters a part of the garden then he hands the watering can to Muri to take his turn.

The watering can is very heavy for Muri but he carries it anyway, handling it carefully to make sure he doesn't pour too much water in one direction. Soon, they water the entire garden and their work is done.

They gather the gardening tools and leave for the house to clean
themselves up. Muri is happy about his new and fun experience.
Ben and Mysterious Muri wants you to try gardening too.
When you do, you WILL have fun too!

Mellie Harp Books Catalog

- **The Teeny Tiny Kingdom**
- **Mary Gets a Turtle**
- **The Teeny Tiny Kingdom**
- **Fat Cat**
- **Noah and The Ark (Noah's Giant Og)**
- **The Bear and Me (Based on a True Story)**
- **Suzanne's First Day of School**
- **Mudd The Dog**

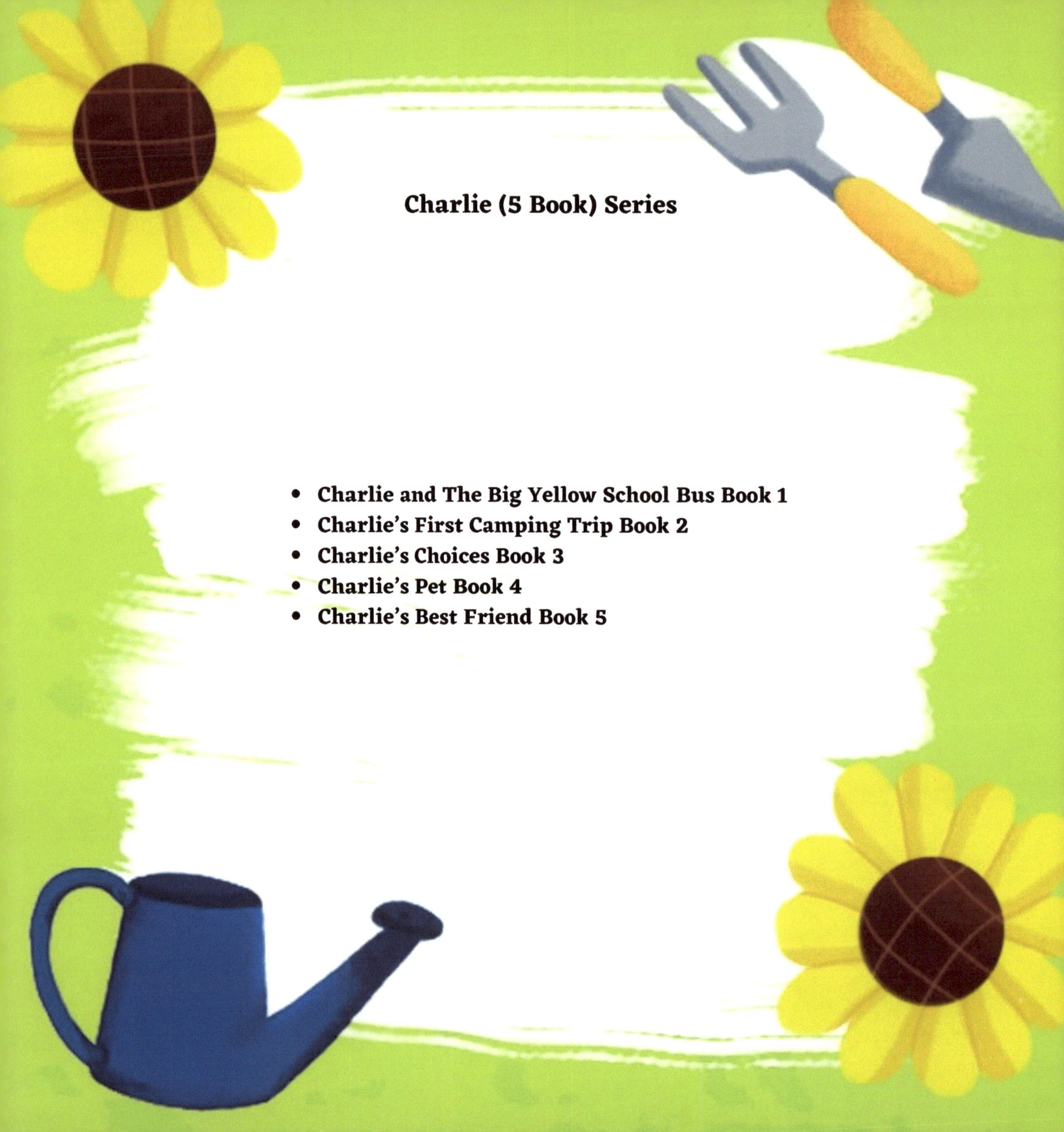

Charlie (5 Book) Series

- **Charlie and The Big Yellow School Bus Book 1**
- **Charlie's First Camping Trip Book 2**
- **Charlie's Choices Book 3**
- **Charlie's Pet Book 4**
- **Charlie's Best Friend Book 5**

My Best Friend Book Series

- **Mudd "The Dog" Book 1**
- **Ellie "The Cat" Book 2**
- **Misty Blue "The Horse" Book 3**
- **Ila "The Rabbit" Book 4**
- **Bleep "The Frog" Book 5**

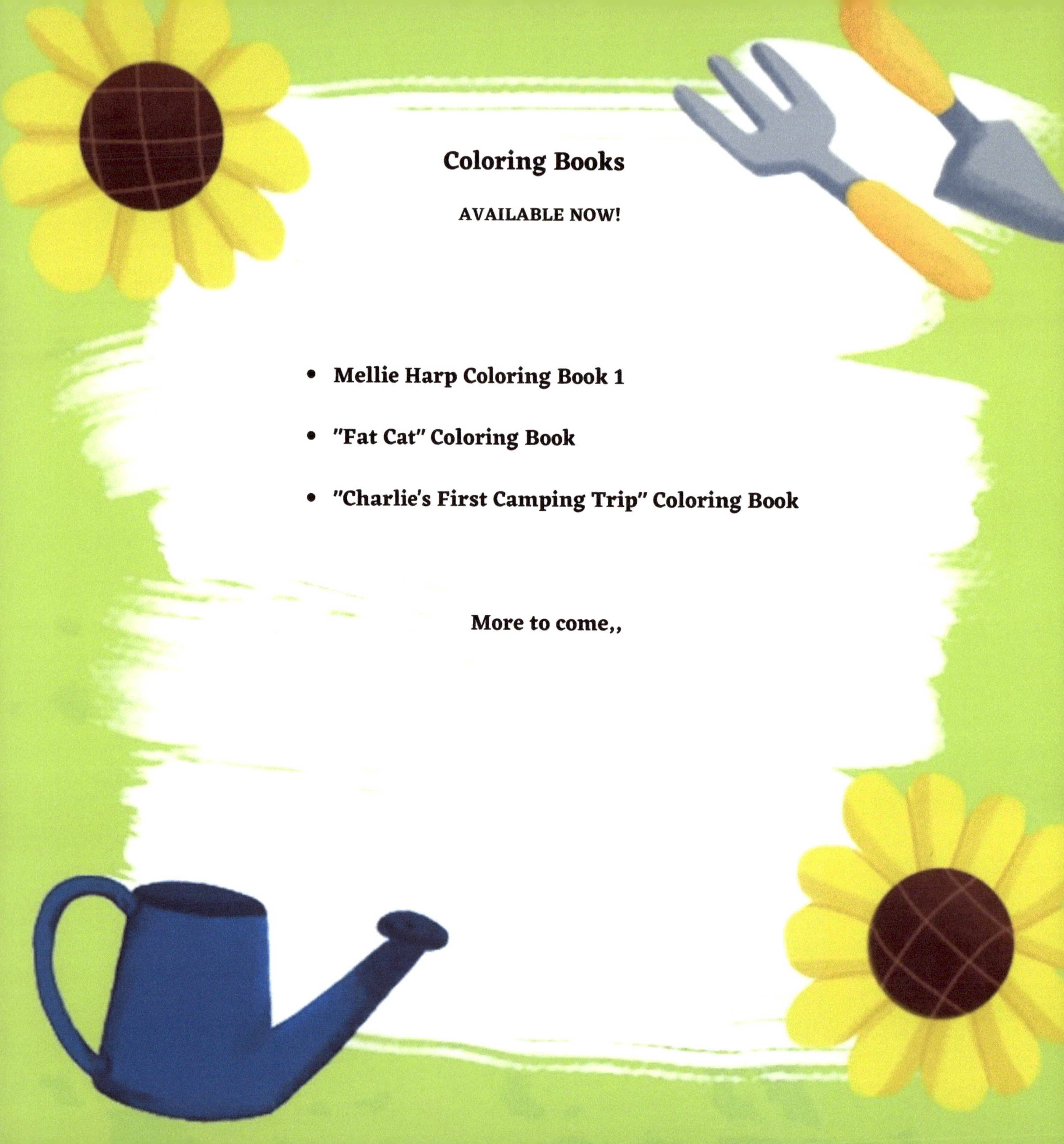
Coloring Books
AVAILABLE NOW!
Mellie Harp Coloring Book 1
"Fat Cat" Coloring Book
"Charlie's First Camping Trip" Coloring Book
More to come,,

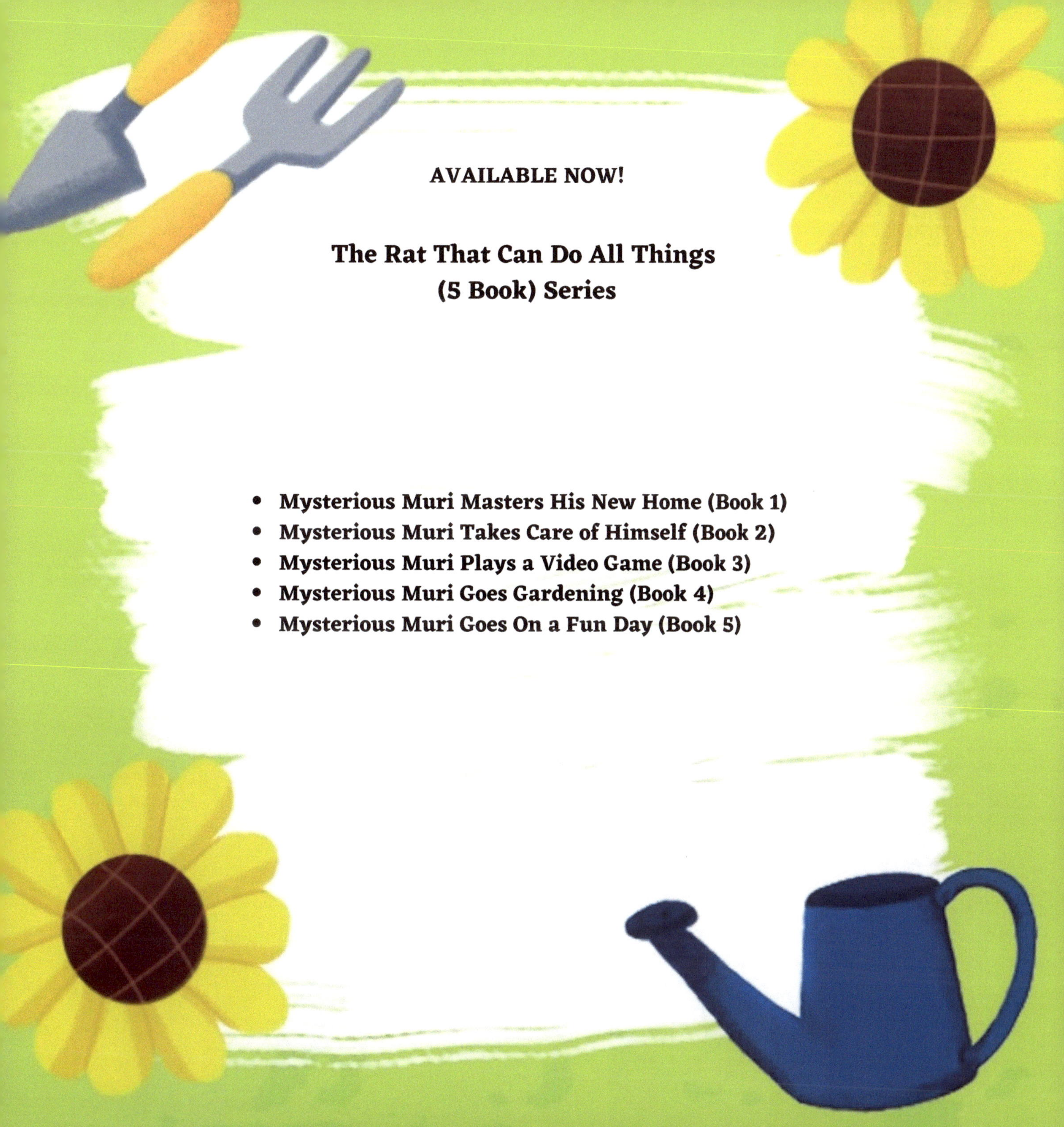

AVAILABLE NOW!

**The Rat That Can Do All Things
(5 Book) Series**

- **Mysterious Muri Masters His New Home (Book 1)**
- **Mysterious Muri Takes Care of Himself (Book 2)**
- **Mysterious Muri Plays a Video Game (Book 3)**
- **Mysterious Muri Goes Gardening (Book 4)**
- **Mysterious Muri Goes On a Fun Day (Book 5)**

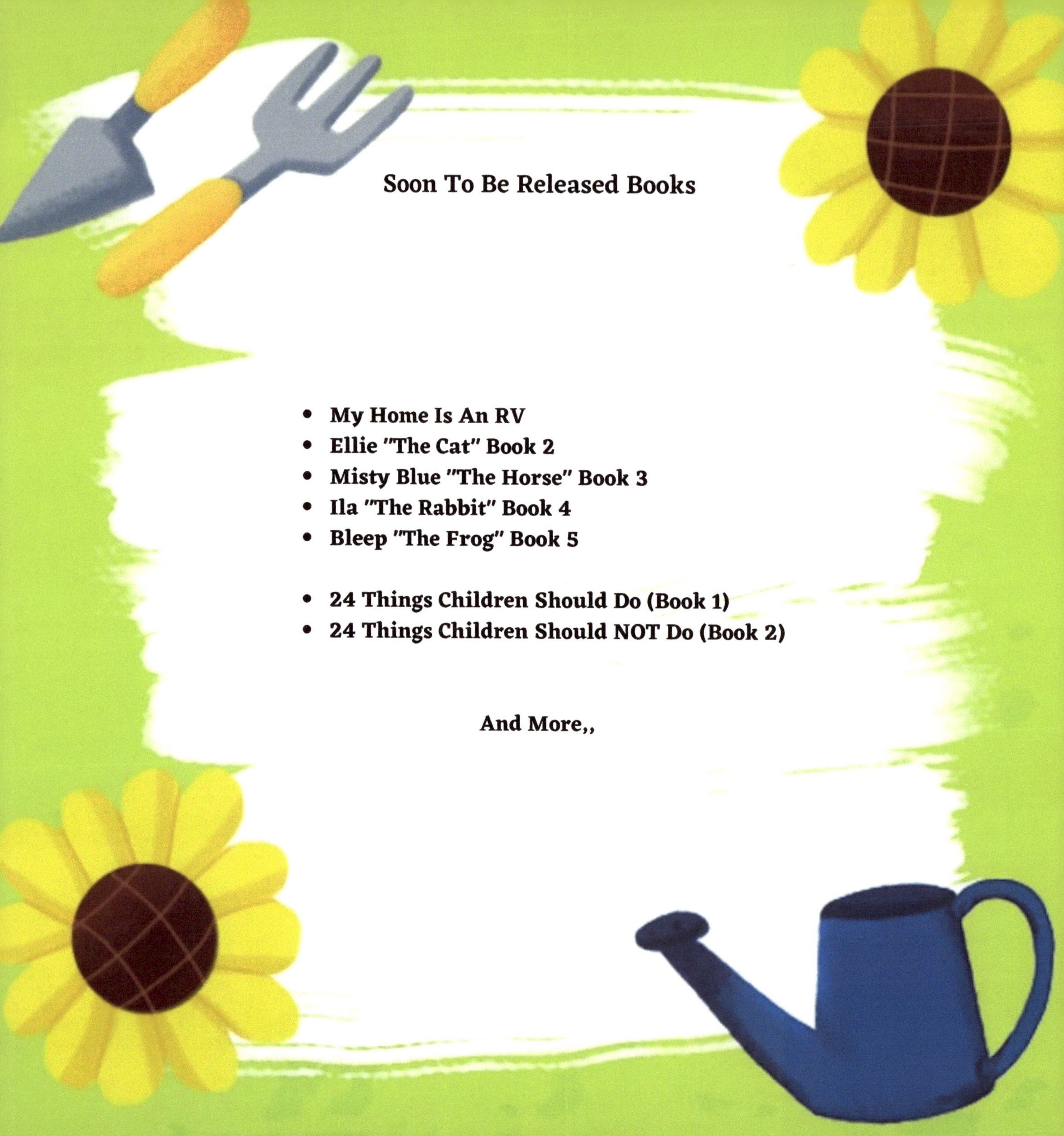

Soon To Be Released Books

- **My Home Is An RV**
- **Ellie "The Cat" Book 2**
- **Misty Blue "The Horse" Book 3**
- **Ila "The Rabbit" Book 4**
- **Bleep "The Frog" Book 5**

- **24 Things Children Should Do (Book 1)**
- **24 Things Children Should NOT Do (Book 2)**

And More,,

About The Author

Hi, I am Mellie Harp. I was born in a small town in southern Indiana. While raising two children as a single parent, I began to write short stories. My children loved to read all sorts of children's books. Back then, I didn't have money to buy a computer. It wasn't till my children were grown that I decided to try my hand at a computer and put my stories into print. It took me years to start and I'm glad I did and even though time has flown by and I'm a little older, I now have the opportunity to put my stories into books to share with children of all ages. Thank you for reading Mellie Harp Books.